MW01287408

It's a fitting title, Moc
blooming morning glc
day is overcast, and is b _____ __ _____. Many of
Shabazz's poems are likewise set at night and unleash abundance
and sorrow in equal measure. There is a Whitmanian generosity
to the voice, an embrace of the associative power of song—of song
itself—to encompass any kind or volume of expression. "I sing all
the time," he says and then adds, "I bury sons all the time." The
poems issue from the heart of twentieth and twenty-first century
Black culture, and part of the book's value is as time capsule for
the richness of that culture. At the center are poems that address
the poet's search for connection with his alcoholic father, which
seems a doomed but still hopeful quest: "Maybe we / Could be
more than a huff out of the glass hole / Be the home talk only we
can give each other." *Moonflower* is a deeply affecting, expansive
work of art.

—JEFFREY SKINNER
author of *Chance Divine* and *Glaciology*

These are poems to be read aloud, to be felt in the mouth, coming
forth on the tongue, and through strong teeth. They are totally
made of sound. Phillip Shabazz is a master of image collision and
word surprise. The journey itself, poem to poem, is quiet to loud,
push to pull, shove and halt, fly and fall. Along the way, we meet
his muses by the river: the poet's homeboy Ali, Ella Baker, Fannie
Lou Hamer, Georgia O'Keefe, Josephine Baker, Langston Hughes,
Colin Kaepernik, June Jordan, Tamir Rice, George Floyd, and the
poet's long-departed father who looms just around the corner.
Throughout, blooming moonflowers open on vines that wrap
and twine the seasons and stories, scented white flags that never
surrender to the night.

—GEORGANN EUBANKS
author of *Rural Astronomy*

Compelling and remarkably honest, *Moonflower* investigates
both the softer and sharper edges of our unique emotional
landscapes in a series of exciting, accessible poems that explore
equally the strengths and frailties of the human condition in its
varied aspects—personal identity, grief, relationships, family,

and slowly mending hearts. Weaving together universal, open-hearted narratives into a poignant collection, *Moonflower* is both intellectually stimulating and emotionally engaging, reminding us of the beautiful complexities of being human.

—JOHN SIBLEY WILLIAMS
author of *As One Fire Consumes Another*

Phillip Shabazz's new volume of poetry, *Moonflower*, is in every way intoxicating and mysterious as the night-blooming flower from which it borrows its title—and, indeed, the exotic bloom is a luminous beating trope throughout these prayerful, sensual narratives where "Language is a saint suffering thorns," and "the future— / a burning hole in the heart of an angel in the rain." *Moonflower* is a marvel—requiem and resurrection: with mage-like finesse, Shabazz summons the dead and electrifies the living.

—JOSEPH BATHANTI
North Carolina Poet Laureate (2012–14)
and author of *The 13th Sunday after Pentecost*

Moonflower

Phillip Shabazz

Fernwood
PRESS

Moonflower

Fernwood Press
Newberg, Oregon
www.fernwoodpress.com

Printed in the United States of America

Cover and page design: Eric Muhr
Cover photo: Beverly Donnor
Author photo: Janet Jennings

ISBN 978-1-59498-170-8

to Beverly

Contents

At the Riverfront

Language is a saint suffering thorns
the way a vessel hardens the river between our toes.
When the water of language softens my eyes
to transform the word into flesh, fireworks
explode a holiday sky into scarlet and silver.
And we bump shoulders at the riverfront.
Lean over the rail to view the tallest
floating fountain in the world,
its red and green lines visible on our face.
How I've seen, like a magician,
the wet footsteps of a saint walk
on the backs of countless waves as
sailboats moor for the night, bound
to wooden posts on the boardwalk.
When the river falls on a halo, her sparkle,
a fire spot fading in the pore of air,
only a true believer can engage
her soot-beaten house of light.
Walk with her on the deepest end of water
seen as memory. Walk her bloated bridge.
It's Juneteenth. Our thrill-seeking kicks off
a celebration under a jackpot moon. I am open
to the river where words began
and language is a saint suffering thorns.
Skyscrapers shade the belvedere
coffee shops and diners in restaurants
while the bandstand blares a jazz-bent ragtime
which makes me hungry for the night.

King of the World

~ *for Muhammad Ali*

Nappy hair tumbles to the floor.
Scissors in V-shapes, voices swell. The barber
stands in the crowded shop to trim my
curls as I sit in the chair facing the mirror.
Hear the news about our king of the world.
Heartbeats stop. Someone says champ is gone.

Air raises the bay rum. Champ is gone
and hair piles atop the shine off the floor.
June voices carry our king of the world.
His exit was a question of *when* to the barber.
The electric clipper buzzes in the mirror.
I miss brothers like Ali, he says and parts my

hair into quadrants. A towel around my
shoulders, the clipper buzzes. Champ is gone
like a dream. I don't look the same in the mirror.
Hair rolls down the barbershop cape to the floor.
In the aftershock of blow-dryers and voices, the barber
says it's after the end of the world.

On the razor, a butterfly, our king of the world,
lifts its wings. Uncertainty rises in my
mind, lifts its flashing bulletin to the barber,
how a body blow drops a man to his knees, gone.
He hangs on and mentions that the floor
needs cleaning and turns my face to the mirror.

I see a father and a little boy in the mirror.
The boy runs in muddy shoes. His world
is the father who chases him across the floor
and apologizes for the mud. I swivel my
chair round to the boy while the champ is gone.
Watch him giggle mud pies at the barber.

In the street, fans chant *Ali, Ali* as the barber
finishes trimming my hair in the mirror.
Sunlight clears the barbershop window. Gone
is the champ, our king of the world,
into the great silence beyond my
bed-less blossoms of hair on the floor.

Champ is gone, our king of the world.
The barber inspects my haircut, and in the mirror,
my eye catches the smiling little boy on the floor.

Of the Water

My mother means well as she holds me, wrapped
in a white blanket afloat in her arms between
the Baptist congregation and water in the church's baptismal.
She wants to secure me a home in heaven.
Save me from the bloodless hole of fire.

I watch her usher me down the aisle to the pastor
in a black robe with red crosses. He opens his mouth.
Words envelop in a prayer. He pours the water, drip by drip
from his hand, baptizing me in the name of the Father, the Son,
and the Holy Ghost—a baptism without mentioning the Great
        Mother.

I don't hear her name called from the burning bush.
Her melody not even a whisper from the old songs
servants and saints sang under the Tree of Life.
No coins tithed in her name from Judea blossoms
or the raised bimahs in Jerusalem.
No homily on her rising from the grave among scorpions.

She's not listed as grand matriarch in my rite, my circle.
Nor spoken for by the Gospels. Still, she flows water beneath the skin.
Let the heart beat blood to breath.
Let the body live each day; die each night, to live again.

She flows without noise over cotton, unwashed clothes,
over potteries, stained-glass angels in the windows of Zion Baptist.
Her rain cools the cows and goats, hypertension, and hormones.
Perhaps her skin flows too beautiful to be seen on the surface,
too lovely for the Bible-believing disciples sitting on the pews.
Her water releases their prayer to the common houses
surrounding the church arisen on Sunday.

It's too hard to pen her to the Ohio River, or a fishing boat,
spear, hook, a frozen net from a winter night
on ice that does not move.

She plays no favorites, shuns boundaries,
does not limit her language to one landscape,
nor to the handwritten Aramaic, one scripture,
or one John the Baptist napping in his tent.

She flows over the dance and bed
Salome and Herod share. Not sex alone, but the fountainhead
sins of a body exiled from the house
to the stones thrown by men.

A sea in the baptismal, she's too nimble, too wide
to be contained by narrow vows of clerics.

Because she has no other way out, she lets herself flow
time immemorial into all hands,
all mouths open or closed.

I cry out to her, tears on the blanket in my mother's arms.
The pastor's Holy Trinity moment,
words that began in prayer end
as the water flows over my head, free as light.

In Memoriam to My Sister Mildred

And I heard you are here, somewhere in the street,
like the hum that buzzes from the moon at night,
and in the cocoa eyes picking out shoes at the store,
and in the light that smiles at people packed at the bus stop,
and in the melting mirror, and *hey, what's up*.
You in the swirl of stars dwelling in words, windy
and wild on the blue echoes of morning.
You in my telephone numbers,
and in a black pair of gloves and pink blouse.
I am happy, Mildred, on account of you.
So, I'll turn up for chocolates and go head over heels when
I stop at the corner you used to walk to.
Listen to the songs you sang.
Share the burgers and fries you used to eat.
Stand in the rain you prayed for
since I heard you are here,
somewhere in the hand I still hold,
somewhere in a car crossing the bridge,
somewhere outside of time, but more than a memory,
because when I think of you, I always find a window
that remembers the sun on your face.

Moonflower Offering

After dusk, you see me open, look at me bloom
on a lattice amid the bougainvillea and jasmine
grounded in pots, before dawn, the frills of a garden.
The days I'm closed, you help me grow,
cherish my charm, florescent wreath framed white
with mulberry silk eyelashes, crème de la crème
blossoms stay as long as my nectar stays in bliss.
You choose me, and I give myself to you,
though we only connect for a moment. What better way
to show thanks than to make this offering. What better
gesture to make than to uphold this juncture in our hands,
and fill the roaming eye up with the side of us that's blameless.
Tonight, as you watch me flowering among the seedpods
and stems, you think of your sister carried from the morgue
to the funeral home, her flowers near the casket,
then you head to bed following her burial, and the flowers
disappear into your eyes, their off light, her absence.
How lovely by nature a flower lives on, even when
a black scarf eclipses a face. For the flower I am,
weighs in on darkness, climbing to the moon, a comer-by-night
appearing in the silence, I couldn't hold back
after your sister spoke to you for the last time
the way I hoard this wee hour vanishing
into the surge of sunrise.

Listening to Langston

Today you will write about lights, he says.
I have pencils, notebook paper, and a folder.
I trail the florescent light on his little hand as he
lifts a marker to write *poetry notes* across the board.
Fog light breaks without breaking the window.
Sunlight whispers from shrimp boat nets docked in marshes.
Southern yellow pines climb into nudeness, earthlight.
He says a rainbow touched his poems
during the Renaissance decades ago in Harlem.
I wonder. Such light could bring back a rebirth.
Take away the *color line* he found fixed at his feet.
This light remains still visible, long after the merchant marine
and river light days he walked along the shore.
Filaments burn out in his light bulbs, like memories.
Diffused light turns round on a turtle shell. Stars scatter.
Dusk releases the day's end into an indigo sky.
When light warms the room, we are its souls.
And when our shadows leave the body
to return in another light, we waken
from a heartbroken night in another room.
Revel that the streetlight isn't a police shooting, a bomb threat,
a poorhouse, a drive-by. *I, too, sing America*, he says.
Sand lightens the town where gulls form colonies for defense.
Lamps shine at sea level. Waves land and go in lines
sapphire and salt. Its voice makes music on Langston's voice:
Life is for the living. Death is for the dead.

Gratitude

Soul-eyed goodness. We give thanks for laughs and talk at our
dinner table. The forks between our fingers over broiled salmon
wild-caught from Alaska. Greens in our salad, butter cauliflower,
and lime-brushed avocado on our plates. No clumped February frost

but bowls of vanilla ice cream. Temples of smile, we sing for pleasure
while our eyes shine warmth when we sit on the couch by the
    fireplace
and a barred owl hoots its airy vowel mating call through trees,
wind-bent giants. How those wild horses on the beach in Corolla

nod to us from their mysterious gazes, their eyes, tolerance
of the sea. Our lodge at a noisy Manteo inn, let us relish the Atlantic
inlet heathers, thistles, peace lilies en masse. Such moments rainbow
our memories. Sail us into the future. Songs to silence. Names to
    fate.

Nights to moonflower. We delight at the rose finches
visiting the bird feeder to feast without our consent. Fauna paw
    prints,
flora assemblages land summer in our lap—*summum bonum.*
We don't know where to go without green-lit hills and trees.

Please excuse our leaving the house to wade into the world,
thinking only of our trip while concrete faces frown from the road
and gray through shadows, defy the daylight the way the serpent
of ancient myth in Egypt, Apophis, shut the door,

closed the curtain to block out the sun and stars, ships in the sky
roaming adornment, genesis, raison d'être. Pardon us. We are slow,
half awake, too old to jump in a fight to a drumbeat diminished
by scratched money. We could spend a lifetime stuck

at our own roadblocks. But we move toward a book. The pages
turn for us. Black-lettered poem or prose pressed into light.
Spill out, spell out things to go with our matter of taste.
This is how we summon the nondogmatic spirit. Wipe sweat off

the forehead. Let the white cloth yield to Beatitudes. Blessings
we have seen yield to *Amen*. Inch into *Hallelujah*. Yield the go-ahead
beyond Sweet Daddy Grace, Father Divine, their Decalogue to decode,
their stain-glass icons glistening the Cross. Christ, angel, a
    tear-streaked

face, Mary, mother of holy monuments. We stand amazed,
lifted by songs, by so many harmonies of verse and voice we come
    from,
even the violets dance purple over the painted pots. We celebrate
the countryside and the coast washed by the water of summer

rainfall outside our window, where a snowy egret perches like a puff
of cloud on the wooden bridge at Oak Island. And how on our stroll
past the pink mansion in Black Mountain, we can hear whispers
from the pink house, or the house whispering pink into the Pisgah
    air,

and the parkway leading us to the childhood home of Nina Simone
whose blues bless our walk up to her front porch where
the three-room clapboard cabin sags like a nest without a bird.
We could complain, but give thanks to the feathered-hair shaman

we love but have not met at her outlook in Appalachia,
to engage the rattle and medicine bundle she'd place on our belly,
a crystal to induce us into a trance on a floor outside of time.
Cut the cord to separate what we touch and what we do not touch—

a trance to remove any off-course water from our water
without cloth or theology, how earth heals earth, and fire cooks
up elixirs from sap: *see, see rider, see what you have done*
to dissolve our despair and let us take part in the endless journey.

Machiavelli

Here the foot soldiers jostle for a top spot
at the table in the temple. I only visit to pray.
I've been silenced for being a bad believer.
The faces seen through windows, the mouths open,
each one unwritten like whispers circulating a family secret.
To my father who has left me sitting on the stairs,
to the priest who promises paradise if I stay,
I am a lamplight in the summer sunset.
I am Machiavelli standing in the lamplight.
Since my return, on this evening I see
my father in Machiavelli the way a lamp
shows a kid clicking it off. Within the halls
raw bitterness and a mafia of stares spread grins
into grins. Bleed them for all they're worth.
So many swear words unspoken at once,
it's as though spit holds back the name calling.
Even when I shut my eyes, I sense night
falling over the holy book and other books beside it.
How doubt fields my questions that are answered,
but not clear enough. And only since my voice
has been silenced into the walls our link remains
somewhat broken. I am here. They are there.
That's heaven enough for me and hell enough
to scatter the hush into jazz without dogma, toward
sea and spring. Never mind that I can't sit next
to the man-god, to praise his maple-shaded skin.
Instead, I handle him with gloves the way a mortician
does the dead. I handle him, blade in my sock—
better free than a slave, better plus than a minus.

Body Language

I was born with a smile in the horse, hully gully, hustle
on the floor of a rent office. I wiggled a small space on the same
red rug as the fly, monkey, and hip-huggers who shing-a-ling
us to freedom. I juked jive in the jitterbug and funky chicken,

boogied downstairs in the boogaloo. Its ebonic sizzled chocolate
on the lip, teeth, cream soda, glass on a jukebox. I mirrored
the shotgun, jerk, funky Broadway against the brick. I turned
an electric-driven funk into finger pops to clear all doubt

in the high-flying heat wave, weed, black-light posters. I partied
close to the wallflower, shimmied in the shadow, twist and mash
potato, Watusi quaint in the butterfly, tootsie roll, percolator.
I ate the thrill. Eye contact lit up my limbs, popping and locking

the DJ part of myself. I one and two the LPs spinning on turntables,
bopped the cha-cha slide, shuffled the cupid, wobbled
from philly freeze in living rooms to party animals
dressed in blue zoots lindy hopping across the Atlantic.

I whirled in the graphics flitting around my face, shifted my
feet in lemon light, did a break dance on the pen, anthem, work song.
I grooved the jig, cakewalked blessings from my mother tongue,
as I hip-hopped the moonshine down my throat.

I laughed and sweat rock and roll, all this woe, want.
I did the robot, toe-stand, a freeze-frame pose.
Not into someone invisible, but visible doing music
from montage to moonwalk in the click of a deep kiss.

Resonance

~ for Judy Goldman

I hear your solo song
sailing through shells on this side
of the seashore. Either or,
I am learning to swim, the way an
overtone between the letter and note
of your song stays blue.
Whoever says the seabirds no longer
sing to the sand and sea
yields to a beach replaced by silence while
I hold the pleasure your
song resonates across the silvering dunes.
Either or, I am learning to swim
on the surface and into the depths
made buoyant cool to the core.
Not end up stranded as if someone
floods the sea with wine bottles
minus the wine until mountains of glass
settle at the bottom where
without swimming
I've tasted the sea's underside
bones of sand in my mouth.
How simple I'd have been
to sit on the sea floor and turn into salt
while the clouds bow
to touch on the blueness of your
song flying into the sunshine,
sand, shell, seabird.

Man Behind a Face

Alone, he lies in a cemetery somewhere unknown, away
from our family, from a Jim Crow spell once upon the town.
In my hand, his picture remains. Our grandfather
poses on a patch of ice. A pose so head straight, his brown
fedora tilts, without which I cannot help but muse
on my resemblance to him—a pose unveiling two-tone
cap-toe shoes. Not a wrinkle in his white shirt. Suspenders
fit to a T. His gold wedding ring covered by shadows
on a one-way street in the Derby city that does not flash
his smile. The bebop of Sunday after church, decades gone.

The same spot where he stands in the picture I stand
at the front gate of my grandmother's house. Catch a sense
of him, whose facial lines descend into my eyes.
Focus on his shirt, shielding a secret beneath his ribs.
If I were that secret, no longer secret, our family might see
how he abandoned grandma and our father subjected
to good ole boys of moonshine and armed sneer, drunken stare
and tobacco-soiled teeth who hid behind police badges,
sworn to serve and protect them of bone-narrow shoulders
strange to his ghost-gone gravedigger like a picture
without a picture passing through the clouds in December.

I, a budding griot whose grandfather hopped a night train
to the north, look long at his face. Finger a scratch in the picture,
or instead, the curve of his jaw. Daylight turns up with something
dark in it. Cannot find from this neither deportation nor Garvey,
neither Booker T. nor DuBois. Since I never met him, I've forgotten
his name, but his name stays there somewhere in the same
summon of absence, the same face fading into oblivion,
the way a leaf falls on my shoulder as Grandma sweeps
the porch and sunlight dashes air into whispers, into what

I hear at the front gate, where I try to see the man behind
a face taken by the silence that shows a fog
I've seen in the Headless Horseman.

The shared morning soaks her eyes as though she sees in me
his face, as though I breathe the breath of their breakup,
the hour she sat squeezing cries out, black seas pressed
into her Kleenex, the first to go, as though the picture
carries a misery of its own, the picture a stay of misery
that succumbs to his face like a fish tangled in a net,
or the broken *For Sale* sign in the yard at a vacant
house next door, the window holding my aura walled
in the square of glass.

I guess I'm off base to wonder what happened to him
now since he has drifted from this picture,
turning into a wind on wind that always happens.
I wonder how he lived out the confines of a veiled life.
Did he ever smile as he brushed his hair, or curse the haircut
through his eyes, and did he ever know how
to right the wrong he saw when facing the mirror?

Did he ever burn out like an unscented candle,
one spark or flame diminished to ashes, or say the last
word snapping in his throat, or choke on the dust
in a small room while he read the newspaper?

Did he ever wash his hands in dishwater,
or speed up the minutes, his time on the clock
from working the second shift in a kitchen,
or did the bones crack in his body after he swallowed
the threat of being fired by a boss who chewed a cigar?
Did the stench sting his eyes or shock him,
stain his hair into dirt and grime as if he got yelled at,
put on notice, shortchanged on his paycheck,
or did he fix his fingers to flick a cigarette while on break—
that picture, when only his face was a pot in the porcelain sink?

Or did he tell the boss to go to hell? Or say it in a whisper
over his pistol and smoke a joint when he bore the bus ride
back to his room after work, or soft-shoe, or hammer his heart
into a buckshot or pellet of a mothball? Talk to the walls.

Did he clench his teeth into an abscess, or sip bourbon
from a bottle where too much bourbon had been, and then more
to wash out the grease, the cigar, the stench? Or blow his high
or sleep off a drunk through a bloodshot snore buzzing
in a chair or on the sidewalk, lips bloated and pants slouching
half off his behind—that picture, when it rained or when it snowed,
or hid the night behind his eye in its one red alarm?

Or damn near cry, and could not click off the headache
of a hangover and not tear his T-shirt, but grabbed from his pants
pocket an empty bottle, the top missing like a chip of neck bone
split by a blade when a lone wolf falls on his own sword,
or scrapes with a toothbrush the torch of his tongue?
Did his hand tremble when stirring the coffee
he could not drink from his cup?

I wonder. What to do with this picture in my hand? Rip it?
Hide the image of his face from Grandma like a switchblade,
a razor, or put it in my wallet, or leave it in the vacant house
next door. For now, I keep it while another picture appears
as she rocks in a chair on the porch, how air elevates the December
light in her eyes. I wonder if history explodes behind her,
and the little gate squeaking voices of yesterday turn second-sighted,
in which she sees another picture where my grandfather walks
in the door to another house of another woman he loves.

Underground

I make sure to pocket the railroad ticket.
And unlike me, a sunless phantom seen from a window
drags the autumn weight of loss.
Rain at nightfall drowses against the air
of a thousand country miles, countless thorns
and carvings in tree trunks. Drifting cotton dust
sticks to the floor of my tongue as though
my life could only be measured in the field.
No doubt this lightning is a way station.
Allow me to stomach the hours.
There are points from stars to pull through rain.
Those blazing spears have challenged my faith.
By chance I see no blunder when each word slips
off the page of a wanted poster as I flee, or
the underground wind hardens the rock
salt face of a headhunter. And what of the wet
shoe hanging off a foot—a blister between the toes?
That sunless phantom falls apart as if I rise to use firearms.
Break beyond shadows like a spell.
A housefly on my lip itches as rain composes a blue
song running over my bones. Bullets spill. Hounds drown.
This flight can cut air in the windpipe of my pursuer.
Miles away I hold the ticket, a green ribbon.
The railroad a human body disappears into the ceasefire of thunder.
Miles away the Big Dipper shines in its own rain.
Miles away the crossed boundaries miss me most
when I dry my eyes.

Contemplation

Reminiscence is one way to see I was no longer
the child building a mud castle flowered in berry bush.
Once I ran downhill along a broken fence to my dog.
The beast stood waiting on the bridge,
calm, sunlight on an urban face. Summer morning,
casual shorts, playtime, and rainless skies sparkled.
Feet unscarred although I heard the paws
of a mouse rummaging in the trash. I did not fret
since the dig of doubt was not a bleak side.
The river licked its lip to cool the air.
Once the beast was a river that left me,
the son it never had, the never son.
Once the powder of milk stained my teeth.
I strummed the chords on an autoharp.
The plastic pick gave way to folk songs,
a skinny voice, string music. This way
I let the bluebird out the window.
Once its wings caught wind, the flight
was pure feather and grace. Tracked butterflies.
Wildlife. Once my mountain was less a moon
of light drawn into the circle where I belonged.
I did not know I would seldom see them again.
And this was like the cigarette burning in a child's bed.
Once my bed had fits of fire against the pillow.
The hottest sweat dripped off my fingers.
I, a bluebird pushed open the window,
let in more air, let the beast out.

Of Polar Bear's Graffiti

No lost star burns out in the web of his hand.
His showcase glitters on the bulk of a backstreet wall.
The *Wildstyle* covers the stone to flash his fresco,
savor hope in his shocking spikes and arrows
knifed into the serif curves. A cryptic, glossed wordplay
shows things he takes from it, something more than
a blackout, more than what he put in, this ex-marine.
He lives for a wall, but fools no one and dies to picture
brighter things. Not the police red and blue lights
splitting the edge of his uncombed hair, where his PTSD
ogres haunt his graffiti, deepen his breathing
problem in this five-dollar-bag-of-weed town. Not the cigarette
smoke scratching the sclera of his eyes darkened
by war, sand, and oil, or the scar on his chin grazed by
a bullet, the wordless frame of his near death
face pressed against glass on a road of rubble.
He lives for a wall but longs for applause or longs for
someone to aim a camera at his geometric brand,
an impromptu mural, a war story. He's opening
a rainproof hand but cannot close the cracked skin,
doctored by salt, moss, and honey to eat away his wound.
He shows what he can through the cap's push,
a stained finger. The can eight inches from the wall
for the flair of his art, a smile where he hangs on
and stars dazzle the dark. His stiff aura. His shadow
gives way. He's inside the spray paint, overflowing
his blue mask, and in this dry town of tobacco, lingers
among the paupers and potholes.
Part-them, part-him. Backstreet wall.
His third eye shimmering light beyond the last
blackout on a park bench.

Lady Moonflower

~ for June Jordan

Little wonder she's not the earthstar of men
in dark gloves, cigar smokers, voyeurs.
She has eluded them each summer
in her white gown scented anise and jasmine.
Her long awaited vine wraps around the bronze
trellis, whispering passageways like secret
escape routes from the cage, and hand of Caesar.
We open our windows to her identical bloom
and blossom swirling across the wooden deck.
Here, she puts on a show for one night to bless the bosom
of black seeds since she won't stay long.
Elsewhere, a temple made of stone and ice runs
overcrowded like moans from a jailhouse, while
alone, she squeezes light from the moon.
We do not linger in the twin darkness, not distant
from her mist over a freshwater creek.
Our pots lounge her aura. Fulfill the rite
that honors the sacred soil, her genesis.
Bid her farewell by sunrise.

Litanies

Upheavals etched into my history,
my journey through youth's lost promise land residing
in a single flame of fire.
I chase flights along hidden corridors,
butterflies and bugs lead me to a flower's secret core.
In the den of a lion, I awaken
or fly over lakes, cloaked in an eagle's feathers.
At the cloud's edge, I cling to the night sun.
Chills grip me as the air bears a predator's scent.
In the shark's eye, a moon-tide sea hugs the light,
and the wild horses wander in spirals.
The red wolf keeps its weary watch,
its secrets inscribed on the maps with my name,
chanted like an ancestral call-and-response
into the rock of my skull.
I recite the letters of a forbidden language,
dance in a mask among deer and elephants,
wear claws, antlers, skin, and seashells.
My catalog of bad behavior stretches to infinity,
but the benevolent spirits do not forsake me.
I've wandered too long across rivers and mountains.
They bring my tired soul into their fold
beyond human depth.

Mount Infinity

Rain rivers a road up the mountain.
Morning happiness for us means travel, the rain, pine pearls
in abundance on the tour bus. Coffee chases breakfast in the belly.
Breathtaking, we ride together. Windows dull,
stiffen over puddled potholes. The motor hums
inside the glass. And seagulls, a handful,
red beaks, some yellow, long-legged,
rally around the fishing boats.

At the first stop, an elderly couple waits under
an umbrella, wedding bands and fingers
worn with age. They break through the ashen air,
angel air, mountain air, this footloose cycle.
They beam as if they were made for each other.
We don't know how this journey will turn out for us.
Our future calls for the stars to dazzle,
angle, and line up the same celestial dippers,
the same mandarin moon we gazed at last night.

The bus, like a beer bottle of rain, floats us up
to the current clouds, the gray heights of heaven.
We swallow the coffee. Coral bells,
rock gardens, a volcanic memory fills our eyes.
Call to mind childhood ribbons on birthday gifts.
Rain pauses, mirroring a woman who
puts on lip balm, the potion shines, its charm,
a fine caress she puts in her purse.
Venerate what we feel. The rain speeds up.
Traffic slows down in a sigh of ease.

Ding-dong goes the bell, next stop, two steps
off the bus. We enter the glass door, an art museum.
In Picasso's The Ladies of Avignon, women are
the pine pearls. In our eyes, his oil painting
signifies a breakthrough from three-dimensional time

into two–dimensional space. It's as though the art
were carved with an axe, three women rendered in the dress
of Egypt, southern Asia, Iberia. Two embody

African masks shaped like skulls foretelling a night raid.
Predict a slave ship, a land grab, a colonial regime.
Safer the art than another plague, or invader
seen on television pointing a pistol at a child.
Seems there's no prescription for law and order in the city,
little Manhattan, the sphere laden original sin, a stain.
We doubt that we can vanquish this. Outcasts drown
in the mythic fire sea. The watered track curses the pale
stalled trains boiling down into an abyss.

Lady Luck leaves with her eye blacked out.
The Fountain of Jesus lost. Sin takes the floor,
sin as a survival mode. And from that same heavy music,
the rain, the pine pearls shimmer on the cliffs
blown red at sea. We leave there. Cross the bridge.
The ride lifts our eyes beyond potholed roads.
The sky clears above, emerging from beneath the clouds.
Our faces turn right side up in the blue air.

Of Time

An ocean burns beneath my bones,
a prisoner of the bleached sky over grassy slopes.
I find the endless flame scorches the icebergs more each day.
The city remains simmering: house, car, worker.
I dismiss the poets' opinion, triggering snarls
at their table talk stuck in a gorge below sea level.
They want their cabal to stand as my template,
the gut rock, an invisible hand grabbing my foot.
Proof of the flame. Bizarre it seems, the grip
of their fingers twist my leg at school, hotel, Airbnb.
Tear into me like a swimmer's cramp between the ribs.
The moment holds harm's mudslide and down I go.
Day into night, my foot slips off the floor
as if felled by ice, losing my shoes in the scuffle.
In their old eyes, I'm no more than a forehead wrinkle
between the hairline and nares of the nose.
Not a minute goes by without clouds pouting, or fire
in the Atlantic, the coast, the shore steaming more and more.
A touch lamp lean as a matchstick held in shaking hands displays
light from door to door. The doghouse denies me solace—
my beloved deceased countless as dunes of sand on sand.
No more guests in the halls of my memory.
Dust scripts its tales on empty beds—my hometown ends
and the lighthouse no longer flares.
All my cherished places on fleeting
spits of land are swallowed by the sea.
Each day the endless flame scorches the icebergs.
And the kind cosmos sings me into a blackout.

Of Cudell Park

~ for Tamir Rice

The sun forgot to bring you dawn,
only a bullet sky, a bullet cold snap. Give it fire.
For you are a child bullets snatched away
your warm last breath turning to ice.
This sum of your shadow seasoned to trail,
which trembles smoke, contrary to air,
and past a point you see
men charging up to the chill on your face,
cheek of a twelve year old. Give it a star.
Because the old ambulance that screams
flaw and failure speed a new warning
into your bullet holes.
Blindness remains the outcome
of gunshots you didn't see coming
under the gazebo, noon in November.
That gray split-second which didn't give you
enough time to tell the flatfoot *don't shoot*,
to tell the bluecoat that *it's a toy gun*
in your hand. Give it light.
The butcher knows when he sees a lamb
and a lamb is a child playing in the park
where the clouds squirm with each blast
over the growls of snow and the grass cracks
like skin on your lips. Hushed as when
the heartbeat stops. And when you rise
from the wound's flesh,
save that whisper for you.

Southern Comfort

~ after Aime Cesaire

I watch loan sharks sneak out of their high-rises
and Napoleon begins his Caesar-like stroll
to the heartless limo parked among the crowds.
Here, tireless ghosts, fog stained, part reptilian,
burn specks of acid into my bloodstream,
buttons and strings no longer mine.

I stumble into the middle of it all. Old lion.
Witness the scalded sky prone to collapse,
rise in southern comfort against the clouds
crying haze, and coughing soot, dark gas in the air.
I look at its yellow face, the harvest moon,
one wingless, fleeting flower stripped of fragrance,
roaming owl-like into the whisper of stars,
featherless, disgraced with only one night to live.

Then the antebellum, a windless history, a monotony
of blue, and gray voices, from heads close to the commode,
to little bosses lounging in half-drunk greed, sham.
I use their hands to tighten the knot of a red rope
around my neck and think of their drunken faces.

Can today be the world's end? Ala, Reconstruction?
On Main Street, America, laid out on the floor flat as
a picture book, its pages appear soiled from snot and tears,
pages filled with bloody narratives and names
of those who did not hear the stars whispering light.
There are no house keys or money clutched in my pocket after
they see me in a chemtrail released as a curse.

Beyond Gravity

When stars fly as planned, I am not the bluest flame
driven into the gutter glass of August. I stomach
the bruised side of a capsized moon in this night camp.
Your sea air salts my eye watching a moonchild
half adrift in the sewer-grilled street. For I would rather rest
his head on my shoulder, as if dreaming, and akin to my father,

than strain the gut to hold the hellhole weight of his ruin
by a stranger willing to settle for the gun and cross a line.
Beyond gravity, I say our history collapses into hunger: Icarus's
counterpart and shout heard from the cars. No wonder words
rise from the written signs with painted symbols of this march.
How marvelous to be musical instead of plywood boarded

on doors, on windows against the bricks, batons, rocks,
and bear the florescence dense in the eyes of a stray dog.
Like a phantom, I ramble straightaway into a pause shadowed
between stalled traffic. Your breath climbs the brute, my back,
picks up the wind's burn, snatch, and snap at a lonely lip.
What to do? Whose job is this? To doubt you, I am pointless.

In the magic of another city I wouldn't think of taking a nosedive
to speed up my pulse to breathe. Here, the same threshold.
Here, the same mile too long, an army of firearms pointing
at the profile, a burden on my back: This Is A Peaceful Protest.
Here, the roadblock and heat holds our seamless wishes
filling the nocturnal noise. Faint fog wanders up the wall of police

on standby, and my tangled pores purple from traffic groans.
In such airborne gas, who could stave off the sting on our tongues,
or the wet smoke, a chemtrail swept into our mouths?
Some of us flop from fatigue. Others put up a façade to lift
the signs mounted in pale dust. Some of us jump to join bridges
onto our bridges to balance ourselves, by all odds, deeper

in your causeway than ever, ignited by your rage. Disquiet, hear
the bullhorn voices ignore the sacred cow stripped of its skin.
Grease, dark grime stains flesh, throb loss, a white sheet
covers another body. It's always this history bleeding out.
The grass must ache. Looks more ache than ever. To keep
our covenant, I step away from cries that stab the ear.

As always, the glim insight. In silence, you are a night camp.
In silence, you are a flowerbed bustling patches and pockets
of opalescence, a woman's greenway. Your bare glow
deposes darkness. In silence, you share your breasts
of mint at my touch. I cannot find room except here, splintered
and gathered in lavender and rose. I cannot fathom the clouds

spilling birds, nor the tree accused of fruit. What is there to say
when I hear you in the trash beg for bread? Or is it my voice
heard against the hiss of hanging wire whipped into the sky?
If nothing else, I am the stray dog looking for answers
in that scrap soiling the garbage bags, that scrap, an Armageddon
at the street corner. Groans fly in and out of windows like

eagles dislike the traffic. Tire skid. Blot sucked into itself.
Cataclysm bloats the ankles. Paper effigies give vent
to prolonged suffering, never a shield of shelter. Still I cross
the street like one makes the sign of the cross on the head
and chest to enter a church. *What is the word for hanging
someone on a cross?* hammers me blow by blow—crucifixion.

Seneca calls it *infelix lignum*, dedicated to idols
of the netherworld, or the cross around the neck of some
among us. My shoes tighten. Scrape the tarmac that I walk
as if on a river headed to the farthest place in the sea.
Walk the water. See in its mirror the moonchild
who cannot crawl fast enough from under the heel

of a boot before I watch another death on the cross, near
and far from the sea. There is no sea, only the turning point
at a new peak of flame that evolves the dead. The swollen
gutter wind is an undertaker grounding me in your garden.
Glass on glass cuts light across a face,
the child I lost, head in my hands, a moon.

Moonflower Daze

I'm not one to rejoice in the rain.
On edge, night in my eyes, the growls
of bugs and motorcycles speed across the moon,
jive in the sky like stars jive in the dust.
Backfire. The growl hardened hurricane
arrives stomping wind into my mouth.
I absorb the stare of lions. The growls
in their eyes like bugs jive in the moon dust.
They burn the night the way they zoom
from the rain and hurricane down into the underground.
I see their stare—the lions, a stare against the bugs,
against the motorcycles in the dust
as the clouds jive in the rain,
jive in the stars falling into my eyes,
jive in the lost moon, the stare of lions,
a stare against the hurricane. In the night,
I watch the stars draw together like bugs,
and jive in the dust. I watch the rain arrive,
the hurricane stomping through the moon growl.
I do not rejoice. I absorb the stare of lions.

Invisible Flame
~ for Benjamin Zephania

Bells started going off. Not for a fire, but a word explosion.
Where would he take us? Our poet let loose a cyclone
in the classroom. He all but snapped a chair bare-handed.
I imagine the thought of school is the thought he wanted to break.
A cold gust, his gripe cracked the air. His salty breath stunned
the windows' glass eyes. Our heads ducked like bantamweight
    boxers.
He spat the words out. Flames, all riot in the mouth.
Poetry on a dare knocked a hole in our voice.

I never knew a poem could take down a crowd.
The vortex crushed our blue-lined paper. We followed
him as he tossed the textbook in the garbage. I think he wanted
to prevent its dogma from being dumped on our heads,
dogma that deadened his brother and ran his sister to a pimp.
No one's eyes nodded yes. No one rescued the book from the trash
    can.
A hairline of sweat creased his forehead.
His face, the blackest moon, made it easy for us to see to him.

He shouted a jazz bound in Basquiat, Zora, Black August,
Bird of bebop—all of them, and Etheridge, who freed his hands
to make his own art. It was as though the roads he had roamed
were more earthbound than a thousand classrooms.
Florescence beamed his agony boiled to angst. We took
massive steps to step aside. His rant elbowed the air. Self-centered,
open to danger. His bottomless roar ransacked the room.
Stars fell behind a rock star. The whole beady-headed bash pulled us
out of our skin. Daggers flared behind his prismatic eyeballs.
We saw his mountaintop.

We could not sit still in his eruption, his words on our backs,
the reflex sudden, uncertain. His bravado swept us up.
His shouting shattered the clock against the wall.

Each word cut a world in half. He shoved the table-chairs
into a bookshelf, struck by the mayhem, his physics.
The falling books seemed to uplift him. But where was he going?

His way wore bruised youth, freestyle, anti-genocide.
The deadlock, pepper spray, had pierced his eye, burned him
in Charlottesville, Baltimore, Ferguson. Town and country blow,
stun-gunned him, conjured up American founding fathers.
A field-slave, he broke the yoke. Yank the shackle off his neck.
Someone painted his house, our house, the wrong color.
Where was he going? To stop a tank? Stop an army from
marching into his space? Stop the lecturer from darting
to the dialer on the phone?

By then his whirlwind was so haywire, the outpour tingled my throat.
It felt like being in the front seat, with a drunk driver, the shock
of running through a red light toward a man in the other car,
the pending collision reddening the man's eyes, squeezing them
until the cars hit head on.

Without warning, they arrived, agents in uniform.
Boots thundered against the floor. Each step a gavel, rattled
the bones of chairs. A quake rolled off my desk.
The officers, unyielding, delivered their force.
A maelstrom took him down, as if a contrarian was meant
to be shackled by iron, arms twisted, until handcuffs locked his
     wrists.
A groan spilled across the tiles against his stomach. Beneath
their mass, he gasped as they pressed their knees onto his back.

In the stone room of squared edges, our voices rose
like floodwaters, stubborn against toppled chairs,
against the textbook in the trash. A binder splayed open—
a canvas of scribbles, anarchy, red ink.

We cried out, a chorus of dissent, flat, ruined, dismal—
our protest, a stark contrast to the silence of complicity.
We perched upon tables and chairs, too restless to sit,

too stirred to wait for the circuit to snap.
The officers, unmoved by our clamor, dragged him away,
his legs trailed on the linoleum, and the walls, the windows
    trembled—
wild animals caged within the confines of our rebellion.

In defiance, we cried out "No!"—a barrier against their badges.
Halting the fracture of bone, the draw of their arms.
Halting the bullets meant for him, for us, our cries,
a plea for relief, so our poet might depart, dignity intact.
Freedom, his only escort, as we had nothing more to offer—
nothing but our voices raised in protest.
We stood bonded, a shield beside him, ensuring the law
enforcers would not extinguish the unseen fire within.
To us, this was our universe.

The Pen

Sea radiance swims in my reservoir. Even steel,
given a chance, I resemble the moon's glow lounging
on a blackened windchill sliced by a vermilion cliff.
I come from the solitary reaches of bards and griots
down through time embraced like the town's ocean shore.
I am carried along in winter, a slush-piled sidewalk, childlike.
A follower, I stay that way forever, my resolve frozen
in ink, hallowed luminescence. Darkness stops at the door
of my eye and vanishes leaving a crisp wind in the shadows.
I marvel alone, chase the brilliance in earnest, bring
a fire-pointed finger to a hand like a comet's tail
pierces the cosmos.

It is December, the last day. Night flies
home to a wet sky, shaking its hair in the wind.
Snow glitters allow me to stay long enough
to pull away the flower frost and ice light.
Everyone says I embody this boundless glow.
A star song swirls the net of a dream catcher.
Christmas tree lovers sing the New Year to life.
I am a million eyes watching the glow hug
the walls of Times Square. The crystal ball drops
off into another exhausting year, each final second.
On fact and fable, I follow the glow. Confetti fireworks flash
between lip and cloud. Steam comes up from kisses.
The Milky Way consoles my kaleidoscopic scales.
Everything immortal and safe rubs my back.
I store an entire galaxy in my constellation.
The glow seeps from my eyes at the corners,
the way it causes the sea's eyes to weep.

Fannie Lou Hamer Speaks

I light a candle for Freedom Riders. They carry the hope
Dr. King feels for them on a bus heading south.
Yes, Lord. I can rise to my feet now, speak, sing my song, vote.
Let the boss man raise Cain. So what!
I've had the Wailing Wall worked out of me.
Been shot at sixteen times because
I am a woman who swings a baseball bat,
determined to knock down every burning cross in Mississippi.

They tell me the most I can ever hope for is the Klan
and their shotgun barks. I'm used to getting tracked down
by their threats and hate mail. I walk the roads
below the Mason-Dixon Line. I got no more fear
than a lemon drop on a wishbone.

Common sense tells me it makes no sense being scared.
Klan can't do nothing but kill me. Seem like they been doing that
ever since I was born on a limb in Jim Crow. I tell you
them gals and good ole boys just sit on a nail. Keep whistling Dixie.
But I ain't g'on let nobody turn me around.

See, down here, the Grand Dragon threw my name on a blacklist.
I was spotted in ole Jim's rifle scope.
He handcuffed me to the backseat in his cop car.
I wasn't about to be the dog in his bed.
So, he fingerprinted me, beat me, and stuck me in a jail cell.
I tell you that thing was smaller than a stiff knee.
And every time the Grand Dragon slammed the door shut,
I slammed it open.

Out Body

An evening anchored in summer fills the magnolia
of stars over Ohio and pumpkin gourd close enough
to echo the old spirituals. Elsewhere a honky-tonk piano
night spots the ragtime. In peace, the sky softens
into moonlight on the dirt floor. But since Dunbar
has sojourned to sing of the mask his face hides behind,
dazed, like a sharecropper, we stare through
the holes in a cotton bale. Hear his song not as song,
only a field holler. Watermelons weep. Forest water
steam rolls out of the mouths on this planet more
a bruised seed than an apple. A few years now, this post-
reconstruction ails us. Bone bloats the body. Boots buckle
on a fractured porch. For the hieroglyphics sweat
grey arms, legs short of legs, is the tale
we banjo and dance around the garden pond.
Take time by the hand to lose all contact
with melancholia. Survive the acres and mules
we see for the last time. See the moon at its mute peak
the silent light in which we pray.

For the Moonflower

And shall not loveliness be loved forever. ~ Euripides

The tiki torches seethe and sink
like fumes around a Confederate monument.
I turn away from the pole-mounted lamps.
Hold the heat. My eyes widen blink by blink
to put out the night fires in Charlottesville.
A Nazi flag screams in the park.

Smoke loiters nicotine pale
before a coffee-cream dawn. Slashed rain
clears the coastal grape air of August.
A cross burning remains the cross
I link to this history. Stand inflamed by it.

Parallel to night-fire heat is tear gas.
Riot cops blast its canister at my feet.
The raid stabs chemical into my skin,
lungs, mouth. Its minutiae trembles in my bruises
and scars. The blistering fire has a fog-face,
a blood-spilling edge.

When I see the seabirds of Atlantic watersheds
as home, I look to the hills unscorched
by little Hitlers. What's left of the blistering fires
I dump in the trash. Wash off the soot.
This water cleanse ripples with the moonflower.

She never salutes arm raised, palm open, hand down,
a German fuhrer of the Third Reich.
Even as scuffles break out stormed with shouts,
she shows peace, blooms velvety, easygoing.

Post-matinee, no telling how many
comers by starlight ride her lean lapel.
Wink at her melodic but soundless iridescence.

I pull back my hands from the wind scorched,
words scorched over burnt grass.
Silence the last snake on the ground.
I even mourn the brutalities of fire.
Drift and dwindle inside its walls.

The swastika night trickles into a manhole.
When gloom contains me, a caged moth,
the subway train, bus, and car motors
boom a cold manufactured opus in my ears.
Still, she leaves in the dust of my DNA little lights
able to spot the cross-burning plots.

I stretch my legs on the bedrock without fire.
The moonflower spirals without smoke
up the trellis, heart-shaped foliage
unfolds her white windward sails
on the wide ship of night.

America Me

Years have wandered by—
since the last glimpse of my father.
Mapping the road to his doorstep,
I stand to lose nothing
except the hush that swathes
this eastern isle,
steeped in the sighs of surf and sun.
The Atlantic's caress casts no shadow
upon my sky, nor do
the drowsy spans of air,
arching above the shore's embrace,
stir my soul.
With this bowl, cradled in my hands,
I pour wine on the sand—not in homage
to ancestors, but seeking their grace,
a beacon to guide me
back to my father.
Let us dissolve this enduring quiet,
before fate's door swings shut,
leaving us adrift
in the void of unspoken words.

After the Hours

The old world, a dead dog, drags his night
air by the feet through this town.

My father releases the feathered fog of dandelions,
dismembers history as dust, his crevices clouded

on the needle after the hours. Dumped snake
skins in piles, finds sweat dripped on the glass.

Dirty money and satellites darken his eye.
Rainbow or the liquor store: searching wall-to-wall

for a nip. The bottom side of a bagman's foot stomp
has stopped with his wingtips cut out of cobblestone.

Juke joints sparkle. Glitzy beetles deploy their gleam.
His marquee blinks names. Shadowed by moonlight,

numb to barred owls, he lowers the jungle of his eye
from the posh red star glow toward double deck

buses, casinos jangling slot machines after the hours.
He chases the bottle to be the cat caught in a sling.

How the moon grinds to a seed, the old world tastes
sour to him who thought it would be honey-glazed.

Likelihood

Should my father not want to talk to me, I would
stand at the door anyway, defiant as a tone off-key.
Enter the flophouse, a hall I won't call a lobby.
Meet the landlady who closes her housecoat
as she saunters in green flip-flops toward me.
Hear the floorboards creak as her guarded calm
makes my shadow a person. How the eye looks at a face
after seeing so many shades of darkness.

What should be a short walk across the rug
doused by dust in a front room would be silent,
but for the little TV on a small table.
How its hum might weigh down this home for ease,
the way idle hours fade in a sepia hue of photos,
where cobwebs droop against the old wallpaper.
I would pass the couch alone as a forgotten song.
Wander as a half note rousing suspicion, and wonder
which of the rundown chairs comforts his leisure.
Wonder what it's like to stomach a shower, a sink,
a toilet shared by a half-dozen men. I would labor to relax
the shivering fog in my bones. And what strange tenor
touches, not just the soul, but bewilders the nerves,
the words telling the landlady whose son I am.

Lamplight would wait like a clothes bag under the edge
of my father's bed, as if he never took time to unpack it.
I can't fathom wanting to be that hidden, shut away
by his hand. I would not yield to his cat-like caution,
and stare from an armchair, should he not rise
with a smile to greet me at the door.

Showing Up

In the room, I am a stranger. Someone who
sees a drunk not veiled enough to hide the rotgut
since his face shows a hangover. And someone
who loses himself for the damp word of promise
where cigarette smoke spirals upward from a Pall Mall.
My father opens the window. His cough
and dull teeth flare over a half-empty fifth
of Irish booze too heavy for uninhibited thirst.
In the room, I cross a lake to sit on his bunk bed.
I cross a river, its tears, to silence. I blink
away the uninvited sadness. Salt shivers
in my eye, crumbled stone, an eye that does not
want to see him made bodiless by liquor.
I want to be more than a hangover, a smoke, a cough.
In the room, I look at the lake in the bottle.
Knock it over. Watch it splash against the chair.
Crash land. See it seize a corner of the floor.
Detest the peel and chip of dirt. Maybe we
could be more than a huff out of the glass hole.
Be the home talk only we can give each other.
Our words stay cool, stay warm, stay close like
the midwife of a birth. In the room, the lake
lingers its finale, spilled on the floor, where
everything we say fills the space
left in the bottle. November in the window,
breeze dances the curtains. Father and son talk.
The stranger is gone.

Walnut Street

1.

Diogenes begs for alms from a statue
to pick up the practice of being refused.
Anything the stone gives returns to a smoky
wineglass, and the 1950s belong to my father.
Wavy-haired like Eckstine, coat a tattered tweed.
Wigged out once more, he wanders cloudy-eyed
dirt stung by the new Walnut Street night. He can't
keep his hands off the cards at a poker table. Breeze
silk a high roller, he outfoxes the sharks to bluff,
steal the blinds, bully to scoop up the pot. Only now,
he has no dollars in chips left to carry him. The game is
a cigarette butt in an ashtray. What's left of his wine
lags languid in outcast, where to play god, Dixie demolished
his seven-block mecca, knocked down his 100 buildings,
barb wired his space from 6th to 13th Streets to drive him out
of the downtown district. Like a windchill in an ache
his fingers stiffen. Can't help but thorn into frostbite.
Ice cuts into his sky, whitens his breath come the stars.
What strips the bone lasts longer than his time, faithless
memories thinner than crumbs.

2.

My father is the old Walnut Street, burgeoning on a Friday
buzz. Off the bench at a bus stop, his eagle flies as he cashes
his paycheck. Time to dine out over cocktails, work his mojo
to bring in more bread from a hustle. A poker stash fattens
his pockets. Proof an emptiness shrinks like the corn-mint
oil in a cigarette with its filter. At the table he has left
Diogenes on his knees clinging to the statue, an idol tree changing
        color.
In smoke the 1950s close into his eyes. Still, he clutches
the cards, nothing to nobody, clutches the after-hours—

a hand appears, disappears. An ace of spades is found, is lost
in drifting gray, drafts its hole sideways, a skinless arm
which holds him. Trip without panic. The schoolboy scotch
wets his mouth, takes him with it on a ship, a cruise
to a named elsewhere he did not name.

3.

Anything the stone gives returns to a crack, a cobweb,
a weed running game on the sidewalk. The wine hardens
into a stain on my father's tweed. Dust dries on his empty
glass bottle sitting on a windowsill. The break in his
stingy brim has gone absent since the last days of old Walnut Street.
Straight ahead distance is wine on his lips he cannot taste.
A shark cut short of water the way happiness and memory
flies apart into winds of light. His hand has no king
no queen to play. How he won't stop wandering off alone
after nine at night in a street no longer his street.
His cigarette slants all its smoke
to the begging hand of Diogenes,
and the statue, moon-eyed, staring down at him.

Black Horizon

A door shuts when memory leaves behind memory
the way I closed my father's coffin lid ages ago.
Less a voice, the boarded storefronts whisper that I could
bring back his lamp posts and street-corner
crowds on old Walnut Street, a strip that raised him—
threads sharp as a mosquito's peter, the sheen
of his hair, waves in the loose-leaf wind, I glimpse
but cannot catch the eau de cologne drifting
from his neck where he slapped fives with hustlers
and ran game on a square john way back when.
From a window at the chili parlor, I hear
my mother's voice call his name, then trail off
into the exhaust of westbound traffic.
I pass through the green light: a night brightened
by sirens, and unmistakable jive within jazz.
My eye jacked in darkness. His shoes shine
where I cut across the beer-stained cobblestone
to meet him but cannot turn the doorknobs of his youth.
Abandoned, blatant jeer, there's nothing on my face
dazed with a shut mouth gray as a loner's breath,
dazed in the gas fumes, and I am only a silence
he called his son.

She's a Celestial Wall Etched on the Mandala

~ for Ella Baker

That she circles jasmine on a mandala to honor saints comforts her.
Dust off the metal Black Ivy on the wall. Finger the jeweled peaks
to touch what it means to make sacred geometry shine. That hand is
the one I choose a bare hand from jasmine. Nightfall in November,
her hand warms up the high points, sparkles for branches and
        bridges
on her altar. Bright by swirls of light over amazing groves,
enough village green for which Sister could ask, as she must.

Never mind her feet hurt from the streets of DC. Another protest
march. *Burn it down* chants from facing the camouflaged riot gear.
Take off her shoes. Fed up, air out. Remove her sweater in the half
basement room. Steal away from the cop sweat and helmet where
loss reminds her, we dig the dirt to our own doom. So many graves.
That child we put into the ground.

Unlike this city, emptiness welcomes everyone.
No wonder the plain-clothes police who eye marchers in torn jeans
and pink pig masks, often picture in her candlelit prayer.

The autumn wine of wind lowers sunset into her mandala, how
        hungry
from ham bones Sister clears the window to see her likeness.
Sigh: *stop leaning toward noise.* Stillness: *plow for silence like O'Keeffe
into a bloom's terra-cotta.* Sense: *a maroon panorama blushes into
        mesas
born shadowing a desert.* Not the closed gang street given to gunfire,
the Glock, the shot whose bullet triggers wreck.

Each turn of the medicine wheel, silence endures her fingertips
and what jasmine does to cleanse a smear. Fix it, heal everything
outside the window, outside the temple, the holy well outside.

I think we're stuck in a dog-eat-dog, the yoke of a leash stiff as a
    crutch.
That violence bulges nonstop to an airborne rage.
Songbirds become the fallen leaves, and Sister stands in her socks,
labeled a nuisance, worthless, nobody, a foot caught in a trap.

Her mantra: *beware the cop call for backup*. Beware the chokehold—
I can't breathe or chase breath. Case out the corner of a code-red
    street.
Catch its lumped shock. See blood on a shirt. Can't keep the bleeding
out of her eyes. Watch his last breath hang against the wall of a
    broken neck.
Who dies? Who lives against a wall within her house? In solitude,
she's a celestial wall etched on the mandala. In solitude, a fuse to fire.

But this can't be real. I don't see Sister lash out, strike back other
than what happens in guerilla theater, or the ritual to make peace
and breathe jasmine after another body falls and harm turns into ice.
Cars let off gas. The world she left drops behind her like photographs
of O'Keeffe. Back to the urban wall and jasmine. Grapple for the blue
of earth, the brush between fingers, sweat running down her arm.
For the shadow of silence guides her hand on the mandala and she
    sings.

Moonflower Libre

Your door stands true to the spin of blue
sketches in the morning mist. When I knock
distance does not dirty the windows.
Sluggish, the windblown drapes are not bothered
by airships glazing our skin a second sky.
Rose lamps and hand-blown glass
corner a thousand fires of a husband's heart.
In the flame, unchained elephants keep watch.
I could call them a mob of bruises. Except, I find solitude.
You have already seen the silence, wet whispers.
We walk across the world to two chairs.
Sometimes rain leads us to the table.
Another time the sea dives on our feet
and your moonflower serenades the sunset.

Chance at Forever

Winter dust piled into a snow shelter.
Our frozen shack glared white, shadowed by ice.
Her shoes off, I opened the curtains for my mother.
Turned up the steam heater, its buzz the hiss of survival.
Our frozen shack glared white, shadowed by ice.
I did not want my mother to die in her work clothes.
Turned up the steam heater, its buzz the hiss of survival.
I fought hunger, but not as mellow as her singing voice.
I did not want my mother to die in her work clothes.
Home was a space between the bars, its windows
reddened by brick, calling for more than prayer.
I fought hunger, but not as mellow as her singing voice.
I burned crumbs from the table and empty fridge.
Home was space between the bars, its windows
reddened by brick, calling for more than prayer.
If to kneel at her frown meant the ice could melt
to water, then I'll forever be her son.
I burned crumbs from the table and empty fridge.
Sun was a shadowed home, its white floor sunk in blisters.
If to kneel at her frown meant the ice could melt
to water, then I'll forever be her son.
Her shoes off, I opened the curtains for my mother.
Sun was a shadowed home, its white floor sunk in blisters.
Winter dust piled into a snow shelter.

A Gospel of Thieves

Not everything that is faced can be changed.
But nothing can be changed until it is faced. ~ James Baldwin

No one escapes the dirt, and nothing less
than the rampage of rain digging its teeth deep
into the house. Old or timeless, dirt does not stop me
from looking out the window. The one-way street
wet with fallen remains, dead weight points to
the albatross my father scrapes and cannot scrape off
the sidewalk. Mud slides down his face into a slumped
mustache, gate-mouth, bandit. In his khaki pants pocket,
A Gospel of Thieves, the small volume says *if they bury*
you in a problem, steal your way out. Its pages dampen
line and letter like water stains on the ceiling.
After the ache, after the groan, after a song spins from
vinyl on the record player, and how my mother sings
a melody over a shirt on the ironing board, a scarf
falls in a puddle, or a man walks through a flooded room,
for the storm bangs on the door and presses against the walls,
then silence, stop, secrecy. Such hush-hush carries dirt.
And as his footsteps thunder up the stairs, I turn away from
the window by watching him. There's not much to see
except he's limping across the rug to the chair. And when
he uses a strip of rag to wipe dirt off his shoes and socks,
I think we'll lose light under this rained-out roof.
He handles the book like a child and over his shoulder
I read: *dirt is too hazardous to keep in the house,*
too contaminated to leave outside in the rain,
too dangerous even for death.

Snow Against the Window

This morning a man-made dust hides its secrets in snow.
In silence the flakes collapse on my jacket. Breathe it, I do,
the fallout on my lip. Icicles cause caution and from gutter
edges the daggers bond into winter's glass. Airborne, crystal
fibers spike the evergreen my grandfather planted in the front yard
to give my grandmother shrubs to please her eyes.

I wonder. Is it possible to clean these corpses of dust?
I heard a biblical landslide would let loose its bowels.
Let the hawk crack grass. Let a spine break from an icehouse
on its back. And I've swallowed an entire bean and cornbread
existence navigating the blizzards howling behind my eye.
Matchless and stirring sun glow warms the windchill.

The drummers work their shifts. Take me in while
missionaries sail off to heaven. Give head in secret.
Ill and holy, they get away with it. I speak of dust
clotting on the gray stoops and electric wires. Inhale voodoo
to disinfect my exposed arteries and bone marrow.
So I roll over in rags. Enemy law wheels

pig drunk as if porkchop stays a culture on the house
a gravy-greased skillet. Maybe that's all there is.
No matter. I've nothing more to win or lose
in snow against the window. In the dust, I unearth
the heated hunger of breath. And hard to breathe
I wind down, a stem swaying on the evergreen.

Awakening Echoes

~ for Georgia O'Keeffe

1.

Our New Mexico desert didn't know she was the alpha.
Sunlit, she painted through fall in the buttercup studio.
Her scarlet-orange vistas glowed near the mountains.
Then the seaweed canvas was a splash of blossoms and landscapes,
each brushstroke like a waterfall under our sky.
A heap of honey in her old age.

Slowing down a fast-paced city
of factories and skyscrapers shadowing New York streets,
she drew a black pansy, a black iris
magnifying her Oriental poppy,
and let a petunia lift
its face in her hands.

The Great Depression gave her little
room to move while I slept away my youth,
a bird alone in a treehouse.
I lost my brown bruised wings
to the blowback of soup lines, secondhand clothes,
ninth-grade chatter where the river rock flaunted its cliffs.

2.

Today, her morning sky prairie brightens
her pond for fun. Her red hills
and mounds mingle with animal bones,
a cow's skull, her canyon's river, sweet harmony.
Not put off by the biases of others,
she'd rather paint than be felled by anything else.

Tonight, my North Star settles
in her canna lily's bloom.
I open its unlocked door. Starlight swirls eastward,

she delivers birth to earth fire mesas,
orchid after orchid, where the green mountains embrace
Lake George. I'm in the back of it all.

Her blue morning glories hum,
Dear Sun, out of all this, I choose you.
I see my winter moons darken under each eyelid,
as if someone shoved my head into my mouth.
How I am a bleeding heart in the passing of sleep, I let go,
from nobody to no one's shadow, except

her jonquils and jimsonweed singing
to the burnt sienna slopes for an arc of sunlight.
I watch bees and butterflies breathe
her belladonnas into the air, blackberries,
the leaves, nightshade, pink shell
over the forks of branches, a cross, a sword.

I walk through her curved walls of straw and mud,
sink into each white calico rose—her shanty
with its flock of birds losing the heavenly hills
and sand at her feet. She dips her paint brush
into the sea of purples and yellows, bares from head
to hand to me, the wonders of her world, solitude, joy.

America You

he takes a knee before the tear-salted flag

during the anthem in a San Diego sunset
kneels long enough to cause boos to rain from the fans

he takes a knee before the tear-salted flag

a pin stuck in the heart of a doll shatters into shadows
and twilight sits on a runaway river from
a mouth of a Black body in the street now closed,
doors at the game of football

not open to him, as though someone slid a
note under his door like another fire to put out
and he feels the heat break and swirl through his jersey,
shock and eject him from the sideline as

he takes a knee before the tear-salted flag
"Maybe you shouldn't be in the country," the president says

a knee native to this nation, his blood from sweat
his thirst the pull of stars among the wild stripes
more him, less him, as he peppermints the air
of the polluted room, carries it in his eyes

the drift of a running river from a black mouth
how it spills onto the asphalt as if to resist
the last shot of gunfire while
a butterfly tries to find where flowers grow

All Flag

a bloody bandage from a regime
a rag revolving the red cross
an old bleach in the eye
a tumor-bloated infection
a badge on hairless skin
a spit poisonous sucked by the tongue
a torch to incinerate a Black Jesus
a fire on the sepulcher come resurrection
and not the hidden self-portrait
at some picnic, but the public crucifixion by
armed foot soldiers strapped to projectiles
armor-bred ballistic ships
a flag armed with a thousand blizzards
a flag the same public crucifixion
and slamming the same oven doors because
a flag hijacks Liberty
and knocks her teeth out
an idol weaned on
a polyp—have you seen its face with a name because
a brain cell past the sell-by such-
and-such date engineers viruses used
as blow weapons because
a flag bleeds armor in the street
a flag bleeds all itself
and all the stars here
and all the stars to come

Exiled from the Sun

Here goes the blitz of a blizzard at the eye torn
by the windchill. Sleet slams into the evergreen
and deer meat in the buzzard's mouth.
A frozen tree tries to warm the egg, frostbite, panic.
Not the hidden angle, but the stranded. Icebox and icehouse,
the morning crunch of car crashes, the gray seconds in snowdrifts
scarred by soot, hills humbled by the javelin of icicles.
Here goes the scavenger at peak season hunting
carrion at the hour end of a minute, the stranded on foot.
A drop in temperature exiled from the sun, the February coldcock
of Carolina, cancellations, slowdowns unauthorized by a buzzard
in the loneliness, a slow-moving highway of the stranded.
No bread. No soup. A red freeze pop stuck
on a tire as if the skid marks want to be unsung
among the cast away with others trapped in the street where
the buzzard lowers his head, his beak a yellow fork picks
apart the remains of a swollen belly, the fat and skin trembling
inside the body of another body. No one to talk to
except the slick spots. No one to take in
except the stranded wrapped in a blanket to deflate
the snow, throw off the madness naked beyond disgrace
or fall to the artic earth, a wing robbed of feather.
Here goes the footsteps of the stranded. Doldrums
of no interest, trigger howls and screeches, triggering silence,
the winter mountain dimmed dull as the last embrace.
Here goes the buzzard, snapped electric wire, frozen pipe
from an ongoing power outage to an outrage.
Here goes the last smile on a hard face, stranded
inside the buzzard. No mouth to open.
No one to speak for the dead.

One Seeing Eye

Death is not an epicenter.
It is Day of the Dead in Mexico. Calls for candles,
flowers, and prayers celebrate the deceased,
more so than grieve for the departed.
Family and friends parade painted skeletons from the gravesites.
They scatter red cockscombs to replace death.
They're withstanding of heartache, inform him, the ex-emperor.
Candied pumpkins, tamales, sugar skulls flourish in his face.

Celebrants do not let tears dampen the festivities.
The Cross, the Crescent, the Star of David, only pacifies.
Death in the short run snags his highness with a scythe.
Stick in his spine, the pit, a pesthouse deeper than six feet.
His Mount Rushmore crumbles. His Confederate carvings
in Stone Mountain fades into the rock. No military stripes.
He clings to this cavern, hangs onto snow.
His breath frosts against the ice wall, cave art
carved in his likeness. A hole, a ghost, a shadow
snakes itself into the gray hours, cut dirt.
He locks arms with the pale undercoat, killer cold.

Bit by bit the grin. Gas plasma coalesces under his eyelid.
Touched by fireworks, his one eye, half blind, can't see
himself reduced to anyone else's smile in the streets of Morelia.
He cannot conceal the silver running secrets which thunderbolt
straight into his jawline
Circle nonstop over the neglected boy inside him.

A news brief bulges his Mussolini face, tattered, revered.
All the other faces look nervous behind the limited lights.
Camera lens, the shutter release, microphones flash.
Media situations cordoned off by curtains, bodyguards.
Whispers fizz up over the Press's flank. Suck oxygen
in the room. They keep their distance.

Everybody stays a dozen small potatoes, pygmy possums, smoked
sardines at his feet. He looks down on them as if from the top floor
of the world's tallest tower. So high up, he swears they are rebel
ants crawling here and there. Glad to see him. Be employed.
Serve his one eye. His vision strikes, not prone to see deeply into
     things.
His field only levels when nudged
by a child's agoraphobia, found in a panic attack.

Did he forget to talk with the rain, the sea on his skin?
Would that be too much? Or just water full of holes?
I'm sure the rain would give an ear to listen, even to his ants,
comfort the boy inside him, lost in the castle.
The underworld boy, remember him? Underage,
he pushes his one eye against the windowpane.
The parlor drifts cigar smoke from his pneumonic father.

I still catch a word with the rain when she's not too busy
washing his house. Catch the storm cloud on my tongue.
Slang, share, praise her between the raindrops.
Is it, the more bottles of pop champagne, the less care for rain?
He could enjoy it. He could enhance his one-seeing eye.
Instead, he builds walls to relieve his exhaustion.
The rain won't fly for his minions.

Let's say the forbidden tree and forbidden fruit belong to him.
Say his seed. His head broke loose inside our head. We would
think our gray matter had no pineal gland. Nothing there,
except a lost cage, dust cage, air for the mice
and weeds destined for his open mouth. His walls shudder.
An earthquake, his floor turns upside down.

His tower crashes on people's heads. They are ants.
Tower terrible the stone hymn, tower without end,
tower breeding towers. Ants turn into water fleas.
His tower is neither mirage nor stone, only coldness,
an escape from the grave. His lost cause shocks his voice off-key.

Geography goes rotten in his gut, a glitch, blue
blood failure. King-size, a coffin lid slams in his face.

Muddle his words more naked than egg from a shell.
Hellhound, his tornado flies off the debris via broadband,
wire, Wi-Fi. His broken glass edges, loads, aim at us.
We are his den of liars. His truth swirls worldwide.
He does not talk to ants. He talks at them, about them.
Each sound bite reaches piece by piece into the distance.
Leave glass on the moon.

In the sunlight, he demands that I respect his wordy prayer.
I listen. Still no word, just another line shot from his tower.
It shrinks like a large asteroid. Bind no ties. Clothe
the untrustworthy. We are no use since he makes that call.
That's the sheet his chosen ones arise from.
Tired, highbrow, all thin-skin toilet paper.
That's his refuge, brothel room, golden shower,
yellow soap in a dish, a virgin. Water pillows
against his head where he sleeps a greenless desert
in the bed, he makes.

The dead day does not end. It never does inside him.
The boy prolongs it. His pet turtle eats the forbidden fruit.
Mouth and tongue taste the life of the forbidden tree.
The turtle loses its shell, sick from syrup and seed.
Fruit cracks inside him, asphalt, tire burns.
Grass swallows half the shell. Heart wounded, the boy cries.
His one eye closes.

He holds the half turtle in his hand, in Mexico.
It is Day of the Dead: tortilla, dark chocolate, skull masks.
Celebrants drink corn-based liquor, pulque, tequila.
Only he picks up nothing from this day.

I watch the celebrants dance for the departed.
Dance in face paint. Crowd the streets.
Fill the altars: bananas, oranges, marigolds.
Flies hover over juice on the altar.
A photo of the boy inside him leaks out, deceased.
They place their pictures among the sugar skulls,
next to water in a glass, salt in a dish, copal incense burns.
Smoke ascends. The dead becomes his flame.

Moonflower Song

Blue in green eye of earth, life for me, a mouth at birth
the in-and-out of they and them, millennium, we terrible
our scripture like a parable, a doorway to an oracle
a matrix this, a question that, the answer allegorical
back to spring, the soundtrack, crowded space, town pace,
money race, ex-con gone in the head to get a taste
late troubles, morning June, early rise not too soon
star in a tablespoon, a raindrop splits the snowflake ocean
man in motion, parting the water, indigenous slaughter
moonflower rides a horse, moonflower tour de force
fire I feel, night I need, let me look, let me see
Carolina cinnamon tree, free the sky, free the one
baby steps out of the sun, lemon air, pink bubblegum
traveling circus, politic, a shock boy, a heretic
Joe Blow, Jim Crow, thought we buried the lunatic
kiss from death, catch his breath, a second wind, a body
a face, a mannequin, ghost from a grave send, so what
to do with an ex-con, a word gone violent
heard when, a lockdown, a fire grin, someone sends
his boys in, to crash and crush the town again.

Above and Below the Sea

The barefoot woman in a white beach dress
wants all things the sea favors.
A man observes her from a motel room window.
A shark tooth gray and wet winces in his hand.
He grips it as if to squeeze the woman at sea
into a shaded zone, like a child driven by a gang.
The shark tooth shudders in the man's fist, making
the woman catch him staring at her.
She coughs as if sea salt stings her throat like burned air.
The sea favors everything, even the man at the window,
his addiction unquenched, that feeling when
the waves will themselves to shore, that feeling when
a woman sinks into the lines of his palm.
The man hardens his hand, the shark tooth does not budge.
The woman near the sea, splashes blue surf
against silver sand, does not favor the sweat
of his fingertips. She sees him; he sees her.
She imagines what he wants to do and where he wants to go.
She lets the thought go as she walks on the beach.

Unbelievable Virus

Darkness cannot drive out darkness; only light can do that.
~ Martin Luther King, Jr.

Hide noon, hide old purse, hide behind a tinted
windshield to wear a mask outside your house.
Hide sanitizer, hide sympathy cards, hide mirror
or gallons of water not wasted by an ogre or moon
or dirty hands or any bioweapons maker. Hide footprint.
You are being tracked from a thousand miles away.
Hide unknown escape route, hide notes on personal distancing,
proof of vaccine. You are not used to a town bloated with panic.
Hide shadow against the shade at your feet,
against hidden quarantine confined to your home,
against unseen red limbs, unseen spike skin.
An *eye for an eye* more than a hyena's mouth.
A cannibal hiding its teeth more than biting your lip
in a high-speed chase. Skid-marked street and ambulance
chasers between traffic lights and gas fumes,
sirens, or a roadblock. Beyond the anti-vaccine
scream of a child rushed to the ER. Beyond a wallet
or some cash. Hide flowers. Hide the hearts of seeds.
Hide the wrinkled envelope with *regret to inform* letter.
Hide a place called Elysian Fields or Isles of the Blessed.
Hide nose. Hide mouth. Hide out until the sun cleans
you up and you outlive another day.

Glissando

For dead miracles run out, as does youth.
The gold of luck, a flight out of the bricks I miss.
Fall after fall, glass bone remains demanded of me.
No shield sweats my hand. No medals on my lapel.

The gold of luck, a flight out of the bricks I miss.
This winter, the shovel is nowhere on the last deck.
No shield sweats my hand. No medals on my lapel.
There's ice in my hair, I say to my angel.

This winter, the shovel is nowhere on the last deck.
I pull off the shirt to meet the timeless touches.
There's ice in my hair, I say to my angel.
My friends, faces inside memory, fade

I pull off the shirt to meet the timeless touches.
At first shade, then shadows, dew-damp, multitudes,
my friends, faces inside memory, fade.
The moon snores under my rib.

At first shade, then shadows, dew-damp, multitudes.
For dead miracles run out, as does youth.
The moon snores under my rib.
Fall after fall, glass bone remains demanded of me.

Rainbow Seekers

Diamond in the back, sunroof top, digging the scene
with a gangster lean. ~ William Devaughn

Déjà vu, as when she hums hibiscus to our toe tap
weighed by smoke, the cigar drowned like a spilled
drink licked from a wobbling table, stains

the piano's sugar pine over calypsos and daiquiris
of a watering hole struggling to outshine cigarette butts
floating in the toilets, and over the Chitlin' Circuit leisure

sticky with sweat through blip-less blues, a beer garden
tinted indigo sparkles with her love oil, and the barbeque rib
grease on her mouth, the sauce confused for lipstick,

as when she crosses the aisle jazzed up with neon
filtered through the honky-tonk, florescence, lime
and coconut rum clinked glasses, ice on the tongue

like a weather forecast hits wide of the mark, as when
a stranger kisses the waitress's hand, then draws his
eyes up to her face, smitten by dimples and Bacardi,

our souls shimmering nostalgia as Joe solos
on the Fender Rhodes, Wilton: sax, Stix: green drums,
Wayne: trombone, bass bottoms

spellbinding on a Jelly Roll groove, as when
their harmonic matrix lifts our feet, cool like flamboyance,
turns the wall mirror upside down,

and flexes to blow the roof off,
make the restroom pipe leak as if each crescendo
infiltrating its crack puts the liquor license in jeopardy,

bring the funk to her fingertips as she unwinds
over a dish of deviled eggs and hot crab pinwheels,
her red blouse open at the neck in low houselights,

how I glance at an island flowering in a pot
while I'm sure the marijuana is missing by a mile,
as when booze burns our lips like salt,

not much we'd ask of another, not faulting
that little orange moon in the black towers,
tipsy, the shadows surpassed by twin stars,

standing room the night owl holds to, and after
too much to drink catch the connoisseur
hassling the bartender over out-of-stock absinthe,

his teeth snatching the electric air, as when
the bouncer dashes him out the door, before
naked voices jump off the flaming carousel—

say gut bucket, say barefoot bunion, as when we
stomp grapes, swallow full bodies from a bottle,
coat our tongues with the wine to enjoy a chunk

of cheese, bread, olive oil, the way we plunge
this whiskey air into a joke, while the rhythm section
sweeps a frisk of wind through our laughter

wired to throw back our heads like the feathers
of two doves plumed on a branch as when we lean
into a tuneful phrase and the fire does not burn.

The Shadowed

From a time of digging television
to the R&R on a lean couch,
bone-tired from an eight-hour squeeze
I chilled between smoke-stained walls, weed heads,
and breathe in ganja clouds to drift farther into
a netherworld—moon, closure, autumn.
Only sharpened steel edges stayed
and many ice pick scars
from my dissent against sadness
lingered in the head.
The brute I'd become
pulled me into a field of starless stars.
A son half-lost, but game.
When my father and I talked
he didn't know
my blood mumbled a silent sea song.
Almost nothing was said.
I lay back with a cold beer,
listened to tales of his AWOL
and girlfriend in Paris during the Good War.
Colette, her name touched his tongue.
And throwing away the beer bottle,
how happy he seemed to remember her.
How lovely to love a memory, I thought
when he'd gone to bed.
I sang in my dream—
a pumpkin moon faded into the grass.

Here Goes Hope

Until the sun crashes to stone, until air draws back
from the mountain ridge over the washed-out
rhododendron. There is always another kind
of cloud and rain, solace in another sense.
Though the breath I embrace stays the same
one voice, and silence. The paper noting
my father's last address impels me to drive past
the lake-less dump of landfills heavier than
the dead. This road hisses no one is innocent.
I'd confess guilt if there were no willows
bowing to each deep, green sigh they weep
at water. I've cursed the liquor my father blesses.
The magic moons of my eyes drift naked,
not condemned, as if gazing upon a shore.
All my life, I've walked that shore by the sea.
Hum its horizon, a chance summit, the slim
jitterbug blues of our landscape. What I miss
in the light departs with the leaves. Runaway distance.
Even the stone beads into sweat inside me
like breath in sleep made parallel by the dream
flight traveling outside my window.

Night

What sinks into the empty wine bottles
misted by November at a flophouse.
An underbelly, voiceless from blue to black.
Her words like skies fall off the windows
where my father's lips press the glass for a drink
almost bottomless as she opens the curtain
to streetlight against the eminence of his face.
What nails down all lids to block out the sun.
What nails up all doors in the skid row
of a wrapped-too-tight wino. After he
parks two doors down from the beer depot,
his staged star brightens lipstick, eyeshadow,
rose water, while his eye blinks.
What was once a rod pecked from rock
at a private crossroad of mystery is now
his trick at lust. Nothing shaky
only one-sided like another drink.
Attached, he stalls over a candle.
Throws himself on the bed. Covers his head
with his hands and ringless fingers, laid back.
Unblindfolded, he smiles at the words *Boss Woman*
etched on her money clip pinned to the cotton stiletto
as her hair cascades down onto her shoulders.
She tongue kisses his mouth for thrill, then thaws out
in the bathtub, a mermaid taking the water.
Stellar in moonlight. Stellar they touch,
they dance across all stars
and sleep dissolved into the wind.

All Along the Way

Under a sky bed, I think. If my father were here,
we'd wing up the Blue Ridge Parkway.
Go flying on four wheels over Grandfather Mountain
where the rock weeds a melody on maple tree sap.
Sunlight amasses into deep woods
and blooms the five flowers of Mother Mary.

This is nowhere near to being a ghost town
of empty gas meters murmuring
between the rust obsessed by silence.
My father is a shadow close enough to my arm
to touch the skin and stay in touch,
the way a misty rouse of waterfalls splash

and drown out human fatigue, failure.
Maybe his hands would find these moon vistas cool.
Eyes open like maps. Appalachian ridges
dig its boulders of moment
pulling down the figments of stars to itself.
I call it my nascent side.

Shut out nothing. Catch how pomade
wax shines in his hair like a purple
stick of gage sparks when it's lit.
Where we go gives a clue of what's happening
inside the headwind staggering along
the corners we turn. White noise

bird-dogs the channel surf of AM radio
as if it is time to just listen to the wind.
I whisk around the longleaf pine
which allows the butterflies of sunflower
fields and wire grass to air through me.
What does it mean to turn my face toward his face

that isn't here? Maybe he's there, somewhere
facing the memory of my face
like a mirror in a silver puddle.
Even the rippling rivers read my thoughts.
Then render rain gardens of April.
The topography a tangled

labyrinth elevates each green blade
in the wild, and the earthbound flash
of flesh in spring. I have not slept
in a sky bed, leaving me in its wake of stone edges.
But I know how to ride these wheels
with my father

and hold the sunset up to his face
like a teardrop flame from a lighter.
How I see him made of everything
a vessel filled inside out
in the clear he enters,
in the cloud he exits.

Moonflower Reprieve

Elephants do not stand in the room.
We hold hands to touch,
to sooth our rays, aflame,
blue notes on windblown sheets.

Tyrants knock on the door.
We do not answer.
Instead, we lounge underground
in Miles's *Flamenco Sketches*.

Not bothered by the dead sea,
we lift our chins.
See our invisible
heart with our heart.

When the street takes shape,
a name, and a face,
we drift away into a world,
one naked bed. Spread sunlight

over the table where
there are no elephants standing
on the winding path,
outside our window,

a faithful presence.
We adore the ivory
figurines our hands
have never touched.

Amethyst

~ in memory of my sister Carol

No more living the cold fire, this wild journey. Now you
can make a sea from the sun. Smile your moonlight grace.

Your hands can make your bed into a star. Kiss your skin.
Braid your hair. You can sit your doll in a red dress on the bed.

Hang a purse on her arm. Accent her entourage, ebony locks
tumbled to adorn her shoulders. Hold her, hug her. You can defy

the speed of light in your drop-top Jaguar. Roll through town.
Blink away the stop signs. Miss the green light.

Sing in the wind all the way to your midnight masquerade.
Wheel into each card game, you can play the winning hand.

Charm someone in your plum blouse. Dance to the glitter
sparkled trumpet blast for your purple empire.

Not ruled by a sugar daddy, a shark-suited paramour, or a white
knight chasing after your American perfume—you blow smoke

in his face. Leave him on the last bridge of ice. Jeweled pen,
you can write your new story in amethyst. Sit beside

the taffy, truffles, molten lava cake on a pink glass plate.
Be tender but solid without taboos. No broken lamps, no lesions

to fall in. With the cake, you can wear a leopard print sweater.
No more prosthetics. Now, you can leap home.

See candlelight in your bedroom from sister moon, unafraid to jump
from the moon sister, you can ride the airwaves.

Hootenanny, dance at your party, a jubilee, songs in splashes.
Spills on a table. Scuff marks in the carpet as your laughter

loosens the corners at night. Your eyes glimmer. No one
chokes on a chicken bone. The Venus flytrap opens.

There you are. No new name yet, only a radius equal to bread
and wine. No spin doctor to speak for you about the future—

a burning hole in the heart of an angel in the rain,
dropped off at the gate and seen walking toward our door.

Song for Josephine Baker

There she was, hair in high sheen, slick-down,
born in spring, in June, licorice lips.
Dancing, the gold spotlight lit her smile,
onyx eyes. This was her prologue to
a new road. Her humor portrayed fine
peacock feathers on her head. On stage
she wore a frock, sixteen bananas
strung into a skirt. Said she *wasn't*
really naked. She *simply didn't*
have any clothes on. Yet, she danced of
Paris, quick steps, her rubber-like legs
limber the Charleston, arms swinging up
and down the side, her Camel Walk, to
say, *here I stand.* Black pearl, jazz Venus,
Cleopatra bronze, broke the color
barrier, adopted twelve children,
her *Rainbow Tribe* from around the world.
She prepared the way for a land of
promise. Not Jim Crow who beat down her
door with his *White Only* signs. So the
native sons and daughters could climb the
proverbial stairs. Drum a table
in the shacks and shadows. Her smile un-
bound by the stars, spread against the sad
public burden, immersed in depths, we
brought to flower how the sun rises.
Her feathers quelled all limits of flight
with nothing but the sky on our back.

Stone

From an old cage, old grave where dew
diminishes the base of a statue, you break out
from the stone again. Inside the hour and a chance
for snow to deepen the air on this day,
you wear the sun's calm face. Your eyes eat away
the haze where a December sky begins. It never ends
how the future grows gray in the hair,
and the past draws gifts. You linger
and look to a tree Christmas enough to light a god.
Brush away the rubble on your bare feet.
Off your shoulder, rocks fall like bells
swallowed by silence. The day unburies you.
Outside the dark shelter in a yard, the overseer of night
once sized you up—blues from which
your body was made to dwell inside the stone.
Weather its labyrinth of trenches and underpasses.
What bones bent in you turned discolored,
cave-coarse and yoked as a neck
could be beneath stone. So many songs,
caroling outside the door. The tidings
of red poinsettia and music carry the festive
ties up to where full voices mark
your need to empty yourself and be whole:
hand and heart remembered once more
and still here.

Visions of the Moonflower

This is a night I flee my bones
in the high avenue's northern end
while silence in a flare of song-laden air
frees my body disembodied—
so the blue, so the breath flows, unscarred
like a moonrise of lofted light, wit-wise,
spearmint-kissed on a down-home drift.

This Carolina night is a burned-out star,
the sleepless sky its echo marks for praise
the song "We Shall Overcome."
I enfold this grace, this grid
by windfalls and voice deep inside
a shadow glazed aperture wide enough
if only to pass through fear.

Though my limbs cling to blossoms,
I take part in the dark hour, a shroud giving rise
to countless daybreaks in line with each dawn,
so I'm behooved to sing to whoever I can
touch on the bench of an old garden.
Make the mountains glow before morning,
before eyelids open to a mirror, alone.

Letter to Paul Green

I sometimes get things wrong to get things right. ~ Seal

Dear Paul, this morning I opened my eyes and there was
dawn's light peeping in the window as if the sun knew
I needed her more than she needed me in these end days of June.
For me, she's the light of thankfulness. And so, I write
to you in her light since I never got a chance to shake your hand,
meet, or talk with you concerning what you will read in this letter.
I prefer to sit with you at a café in Chapel Hill and chat over tea,
but can't now that you've passed away into the gift
of her light that shines forever.

I read your story "Education South" a few days ago, and your
words seesawed the white space and were downright arresting.
I flashed back to something you said in it, *the young white men,*
the keepers of tomorrow and the burgeoning South, were being
trained in the way they should go—which I took to mean
(what you did not say) trained to uphold white supremacy
and the scourge of the Lost Cause crawling through their veins,
and they were also trained to suppress Blacks. And they did. For I
    find
no peace or nonviolence in the rebel yell that is Confederate heritage.

I took to heart the wail of a funeral song unfolding your story,
a song that bothered the butterflies, or darkened a bowed head
at the gravesite, one long-winded sorrow song arrowing straight
    through
the campus and white college kids nodding over their books,
where a young Black man's life was being laid in the ground.
Yes, it was a time for mourners to sing, but for others, a time to be
    silent.
If that appointed hour consumed the lost minutes, and pressed
into the besieged body, no smile, no laughter, at least his burial
was with a song pushing through the dead air of human indifference.

The end becomes a journey.

After your story, and after this letter, the funeral song still rises
off the page to where *nobody loves me, but my mother,*
and she could be jiving me too. Yes, Paul, the song settles
in another song, then another, in which its blues handles
each personal tragedy, each slammed door, and faces it with grace,
lifting grief out of the gut, while its airborne glow
backs up the melody to its deepest delight, and a shirt hangs
clean on the clothesline, or a boy swims across the river,
even as the mother tree loses more leaves in November, in a season
that won't let her bear more fruit or give more shade.

This is the soul of everyday blues. All service and silence
glow from that spring. I hear the song slip up and down
the airwaves in a call-and-response chant, field holler, ring shout.
Blues voices sing the stories slanted from home talk
of the mother tongue. The sound comes to its senses in my ear
and takes me to a land beyond heartbreak, fallout, and the grave.
That soil remains a sunlit road where
such song does no harm and roses bloom on a bush
offering its rain blossoms like handwritten letters.

Light darkens the dark.

The dead young Black man in your story was my son in a previous
     life.
He had walked in the darkest spots of Carolina, from slum
to dope den, from a smoked-up room to youth lockup.
I'd lost him to that world, a father without his son, a void, a sign
of the times. He was wayward, talkative, and people listened.
His grin could charm a place, but he was distant as a cloud
on the night he died.

As for washing his dead body, my hands shrank.
I was so heavy with shadows, a wall of blank paper breathed
over his face gone gray. I pulled back the sheet to scrub everything
worn and dirty. Covered his private parts with a cloth.
Shut his eyes. Closed his mouth. Brushed his hair. I used a soapy

sponge to clean his flesh. I rolled him, turned him, and added camphor
to the bucket of water and rinsed his skin. Silence tiptoed around the bed.
I didn't want to hear the sorrow of a funeral song
over his body, over his soul out of body, invisible.

I couldn't see it, and I wanted to, but he cut me off.
He fell up into the stars, distancing himself from my grief
as I wiped his back and shoulders with a towel. His toes were cold.
His knee where a scar lay jagged as a weed, stiffened a little
like me, as though I were him, hounded by cannibals
for running the streets, wild, callous, hounded for chasing money
where a fired gun does not spare a dealer in the midst.

Through darkness, I dressed him for the funeral,
placed his arms alongside his body. Straightened his legs
while the drip from a faucet sent me into orbit
before reaching his final resting place. My head, my eyes
began to wander away from the shirt, the suit, the shroud.
I unlocked the door, hoisted his dead weight on my back
and carried it there, across ridges, sand hills, valleys,
a father without his son.

In All My Carolina Dreams

Part of me fled to a foxhole. Part of me hid in a mountain.
I led the life of an outcast haunted by my dead son,
until my own books and lamps, my own table and chair
were lost to me, even in this letter, uneasy now, bitter then,
and in that nausea, I wore the same heavy white coat.
I don't remember where I got it, which I can't stand to admit.
This was the trouble when I slept in an abandoned house,
letting its dampness lick the tremble of my lip, or vent war
on a sunflower, while I sucked its seed on my tongue.
When I covered the walls with pictures of my son's Black face,
I knew anything could happen.

Why do I tell you all this? It is because our paths crossed,
and I would not have trusted the funeral song, except,
I sing all the time. I bury sons all the time.
I hear a crowd of mourners singing in a cemetery,
while college kids withdraw to babbling professors who
still train them in the way they should go
like the shriek of a train ripping the track,
its wheels careening downhill through Carolina.
I see the same unconcern in a blizzard
or a hurricane spinning across the Atlantic.

As for your story finding me by that window, and my blank
sheet of paper, I wasn't sure how to call for the young dead man,
how to act as a go-between with death
so I could call him by his birth name, open my hand,
pick up the pen and leap word after black word
into the white space of this page, with grace,
that I might find a chance of light where it had been lost.

Acknowledgments

Grateful acknowledgment is made to the editors of the following journals in which these poems—sometimes under different titles or in slightly different versions—appeared: *Against the Margin, Antonym, BREATHE, Broadkill Review, Fine Lines, Florida Review, Galway Review, Gyroscope, Hamilton Stone Review, Hamline Lit Link, Impossible Task, Impspired, Indicia, Ink Sac, In Parentheses, K'in, Line Rider, Mason Street Review, New Critique, On the Seawall, Original Van Gogh's Ear Anthology, Pine Hills Review, Queen's Quarterly, Rebelle Society, Sky Island Journal, Table Rock Journal,* and *Thimble.*

Title Index

First Line Index